SHARK

Written by Simon Mugford

TOP THAT! Kids™

Copyright © 2004 Top That! Publishing plc
Tide Mill Way, Woodbridge, Suffolk, IP12 1AP, UK
www.topthatpublishing.com
Top That! is a Registered Trademark of Top That! Publishing plc

Contents

The image of a shark is a fearsome one – films and television often portray these amazing creatures as just bloodthirsty killers.

Predators

Although a few have been known to attack people, this is rare. Every year there are far more attacks on humans by domestic pets than by sharks.

Great white shark.

Super Species

There are approximately 375 species of shark, ranging in size from the dwarf dogfish at 16 cm long to the whale shark at 12 m long.

Elasmobranch

Although they do not look alike, sharks are closely related to manta rays, skates, guitarfish and sawfish. Together, these are known as the elasmobranch family.

Manta ray.

Films like to scare us with tales of bloodthirsty sharks but not all of them are dangerous.

Harmless

Some sharks are fierce hunters and there have been attacks on people, but many are harmless and never come into contact with humans.

Fish

A shark is a type of fish. There are many different species of sharks which exist in many shapes and sizes.

Flexible Friend

The main difference between sharks and other fish is that their skeletons are flexible, not hard and bony.

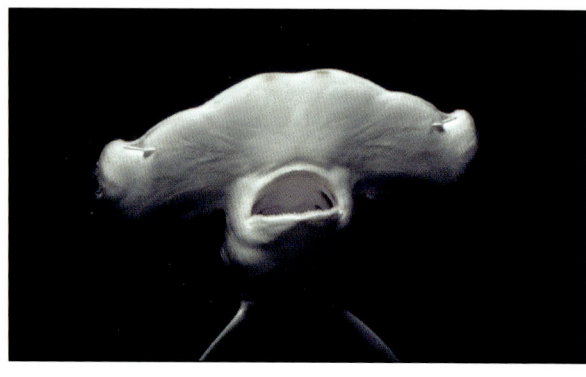

The hammerhead shark is able to see for great distances, due to the wide positioning of its eyes.

Torpedo

Many sharks have a torpedo-shaped body – excellent for swimming at speed. Some living on the bottom of the ocean are rounder and heavier.

Swim Bladder

Bony fish also have a swim bladder – a kind of sack that they inflate and deflate to move up or down in the water. Sharks do not have these and most need to keep moving so that they do not sink.

Spots and Stripes

Sharks vary in colour, from reddish brown and metallic blue to grey or almost black. Many have markings such as spots or stripes. Shark skin does not have scales like bony fish, but is covered with small, tooth-like ridges. The skin is very rough.

The markings on the lesser spotted dogfish help to camouflage it against the sea bed.

Travelling Sharks

Different species of sharks are found all over the world, in coastal areas and far out to sea. Some travel many thousands of miles, others stay in a very small area.

Still Learning

Sharks are fascinating creatures and there is a lot that we do not yet understand about them.

The grey reef shark is torpedo-shaped, meaning it can swim through the water at great speeds.

Sharks can vary greatly in appearance, size and colour but there are some features that are common to most species.

Huge Mouth

Most sharks have several rows of very sharp teeth to tear up food.

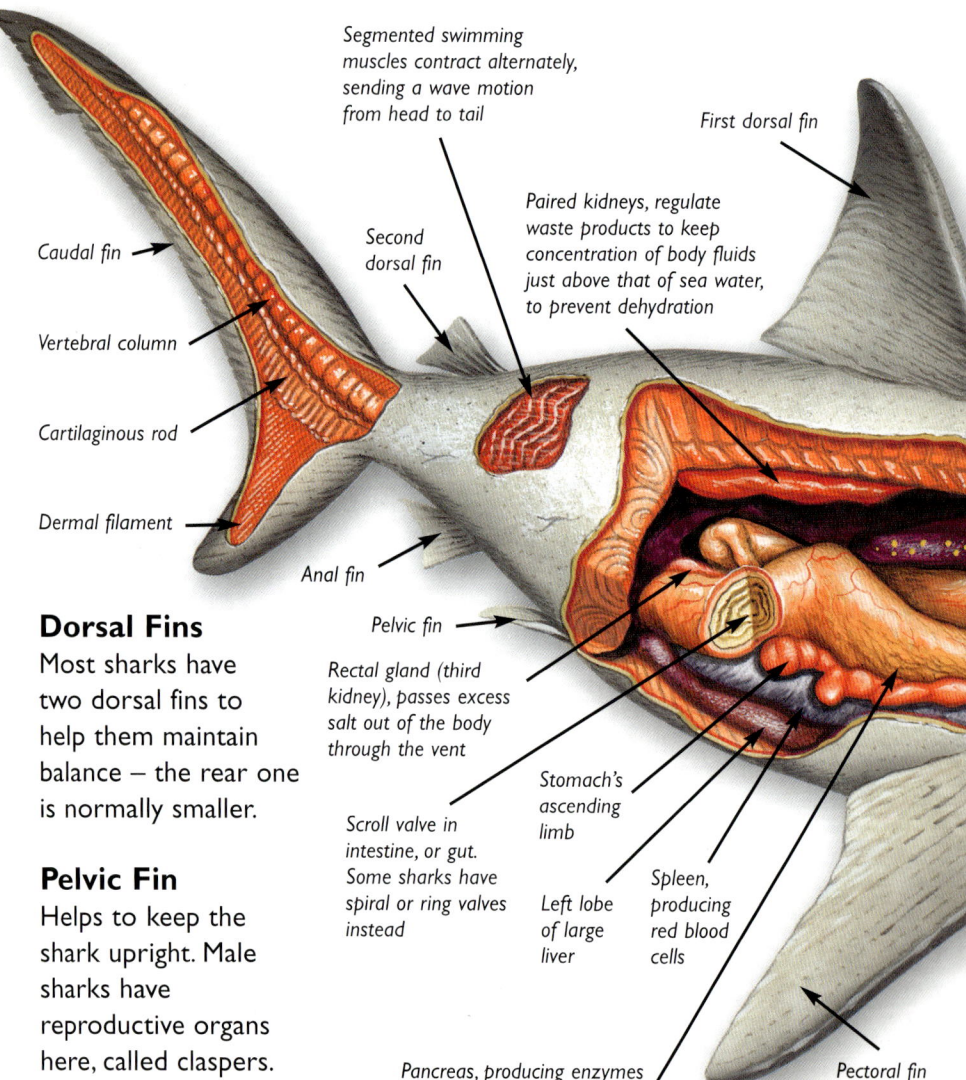

Segmented swimming muscles contract alternately, sending a wave motion from head to tail

First dorsal fin

Paired kidneys, regulate waste products to keep concentration of body fluids just above that of sea water, to prevent dehydration

Caudal fin

Second dorsal fin

Vertebral column

Cartilaginous rod

Dermal filament

Anal fin

Pelvic fin

Dorsal Fins

Most sharks have two dorsal fins to help them maintain balance – the rear one is normally smaller.

Rectal gland (third kidney), passes excess salt out of the body through the vent

Stomach's ascending limb

Pelvic Fin

Helps to keep the shark upright. Male sharks have reproductive organs here, called claspers.

Scroll valve in intestine, or gut. Some sharks have spiral or ring valves instead

Left lobe of large liver

Spleen, producing red blood cells

Pancreas, producing enzymes to help digest food in gut

Pectoral fin

Caudal Fin

This is what most sharks use to propel themselves through the water.

Making Babies

All sharks reproduce by internal fertilisation. The male's claspers transfer sperm into the female.

Viviparous Sharks

Viviparous sharks give birth to up to 100 live young, called pups.

Oviparous Sharks

Oviparous sharks lay eggs that attach to rocks. They hatch after six to fifteen months.

Ovoviviparous Sharks

Ovoviviparous sharks grow in an egg inside the female's body. The young shark hatches while it is still inside the female and then eats any unfertilised (undeveloped) eggs.

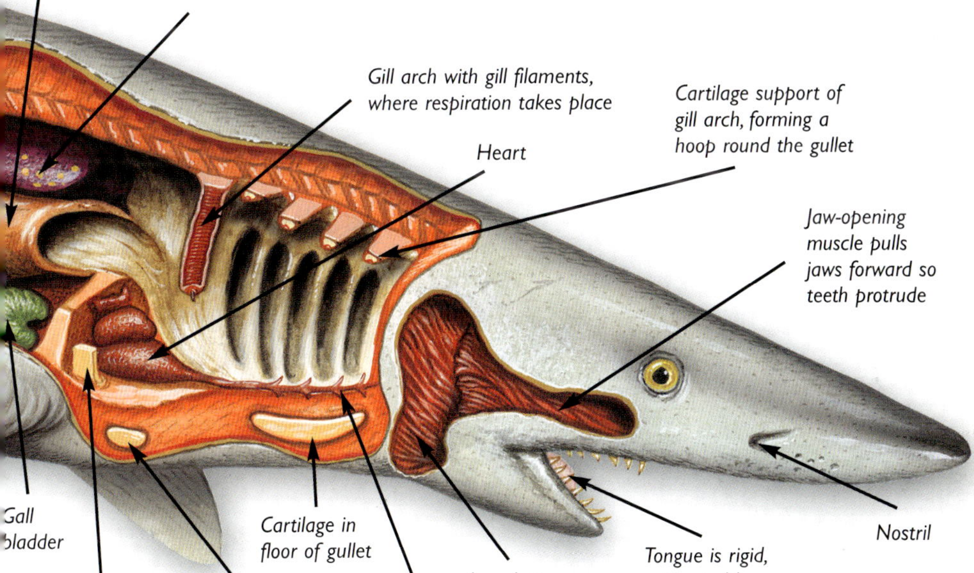

The leathery shell of an oviparous shark's egg lays entangled amongst sea plants.

Stomach's descending limb

Ovary (eggs visible within its wall). When ripe, the eggs pass into a tube for fertilisation

Gill arch with gill filaments, where respiration takes place

Heart

Cartilage support of gill arch, forming a hoop round the gullet

Jaw-opening muscle pulls jaws forward so teeth protrude

Gall bladder

Cartilage in floor of gullet

Jaw-closing muscle

Tongue is rigid, supported by a pad of cartilage

Nostril

Cartilage of pectoral girdle, supports pectoral fins and protects heart

Cartilage at base of pectoral fin

Aorta, with bronchial arteries

Sharks can see, hear, smell, taste and touch things in similar ways to us. However, they are specially adapted for the underwater world, so that they can find their way around, communicate and find food.

Smell

A shark's sense of smell is its most useful and highly developed sense. They can detect very weak smells in huge amounts of water.

Vision

Sharks' eyes are very sensitive to light and can find some things in very dark, murky water.

The great white's ampullae of Lorenzini (sensory organs to detect the electric field of its prey) are particularly prominent.

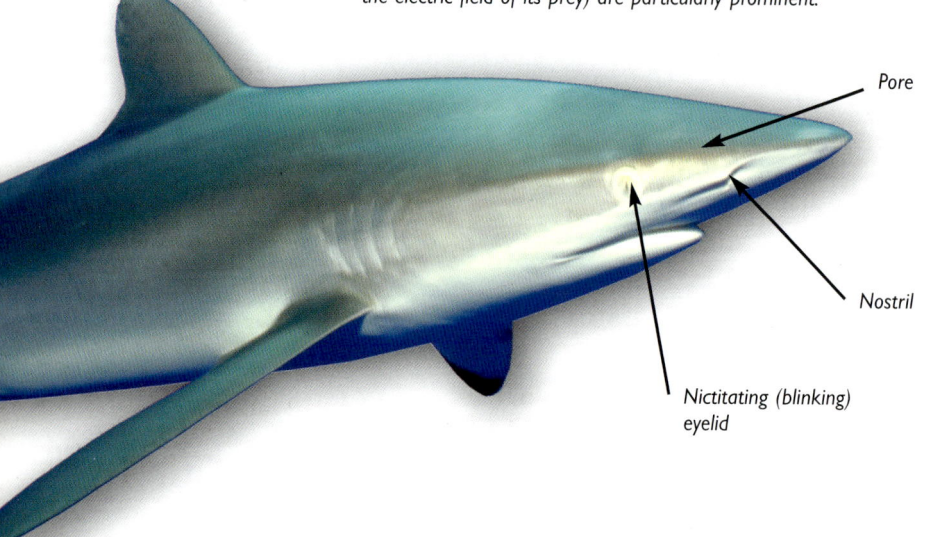

Pore

Nostril

Nictitating (blinking) eyelid

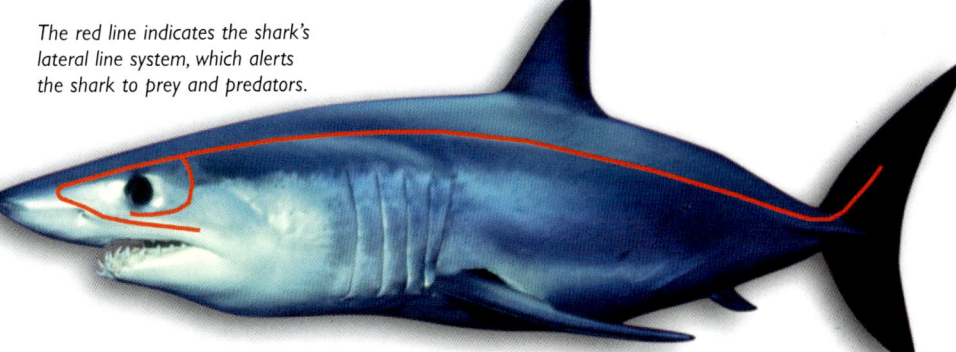

The red line indicates the shark's lateral line system, which alerts the shark to prey and predators.

Sixth Sense

Sharks also have a sixth sense. They have special pores on their heads called ampullae of Lorenzini. These pick up the very weak electrical signals produced by the muscles of living things in the water.

Bio Compass

It is thought that sharks that travel thousands of miles use this sense to 'tune in' to Earth's magnetic field. This 'biological compass' helps them to find their way around the oceans.

Sound

Sharks can detect sound waves and movement in the water thanks to the system of nerves along their side.

Touch

They can feel things with their nose – some have barbels (feelers) that they use to find things buried in the sea bottom.

Taste

Their taste buds are on bumps inside their mouths. They will spit out anything that isn't tasty.

The barbels on a nurse shark help it to find food.

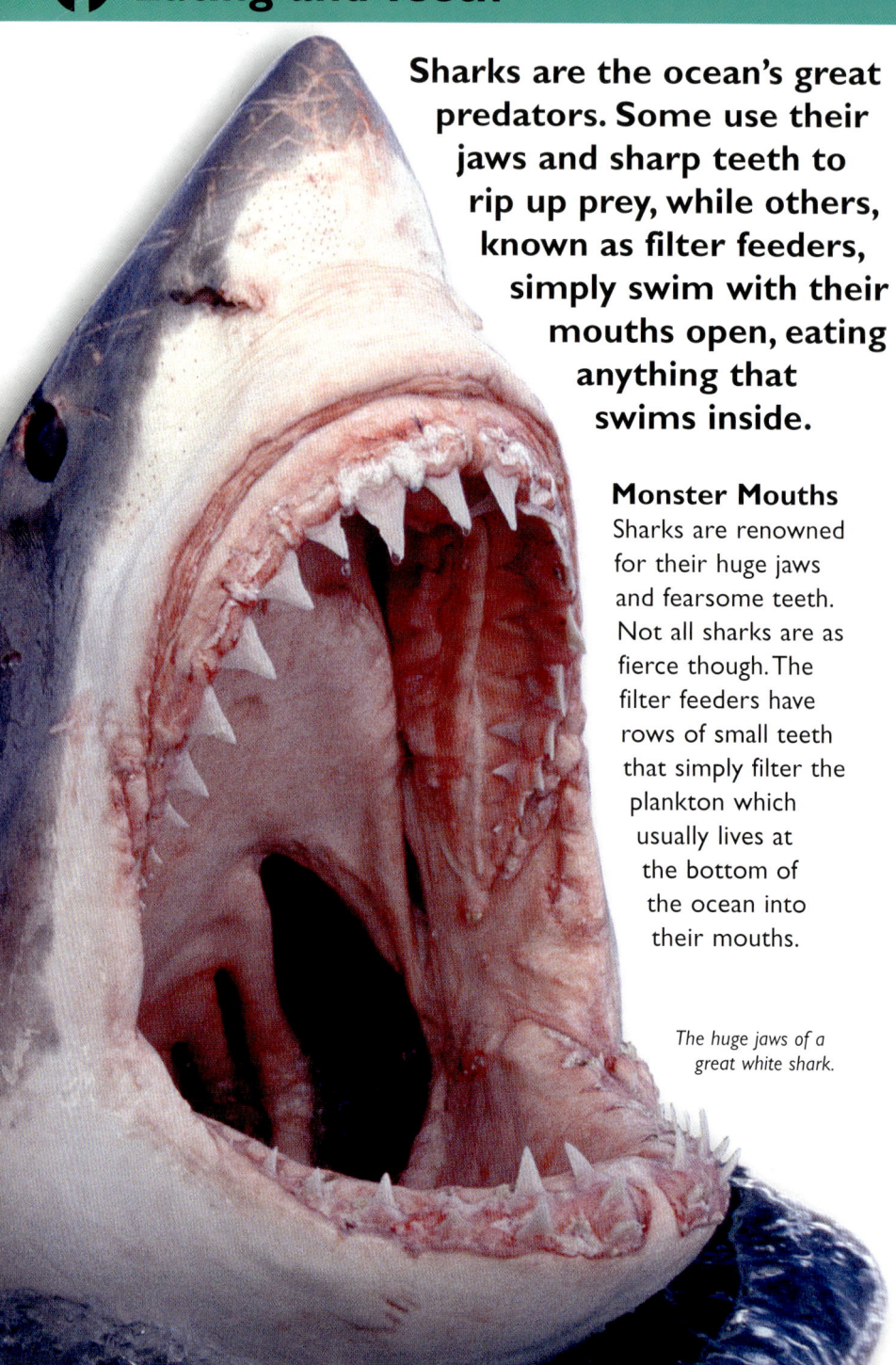

Sharks are the ocean's great predators. Some use their jaws and sharp teeth to rip up prey, while others, known as filter feeders, simply swim with their mouths open, eating anything that swims inside.

Monster Mouths

Sharks are renowned for their huge jaws and fearsome teeth. Not all sharks are as fierce though. The filter feeders have rows of small teeth that simply filter the plankton which usually lives at the bottom of the ocean into their mouths.

The huge jaws of a great white shark.

A tiger shark feeds on the carcass of a sperm whale.

There are normally several rows of teeth – some sharks can have thousands of teeth at one time – and a new tooth simply rotates into place at the front. The teeth get bigger as the shark grows.

Different Teeth

Sharks' teeth vary between different species, depending on what they eat. Sharks that eat slippery fish like squid tend to have long, curved teeth. Serrated teeth are good for cutting up bony fish.

The fearsome teeth of the tiger shark. Note also the shark's prominent ampullae of Lorenzini.

Tooth Talk

One thing that is common to all sharks is that as their teeth wear out, they are replaced by new ones.

Tooth Types

Spiked teeth can grip small prey as the shark tears it apart. Flat, strong teeth are used to crush and crunch up tough shellfish.

Strong Jaw

Some sharks have a combination of different types of teeth. The tiger shark will eat almost anything and has a wide variety of teeth. Its teeth and jaws are strong enough to cut through a turtle shell!

The different types of teeth found in sharks.

11

Sharks first appeared in Earth's oceans over 300 million years ago – long before dinosaurs walked on Earth.

The fearsome megalodon is thought to have been able to eat creatures as large as whales.

Megalodon

Megalodon was an enormous shark. Scientists estimate that it grew to over 12 m – over twice the size of its present-day relative, the great white (see pages 32–33). It is not known exactly when megalodon became extinct, but it could have lived as recently as 12,000 years ago.

Mighty Molars

We only know about the megalodon because scientists have been able to study its fossilised teeth.

The fossilised tooth of a megalodon.

Hundreds of Teeth

Megalodon probably had hundreds of teeth at any one time, which it used to bite large chunks out of its prey. It probably ate other large creatures such as whales.

Huge Jaw

Fossilised megalodon teeth up to 17 cm long have been found in Europe, India, Australia, and both North and South America. The size of the teeth suggests that its jaws could open to 1.8 m wide and 2.1 m high.

Great White Shark

No other megalodon remains have been found (shark skeletons do not preserve well) so we can only guess what this giant shark looked like, but most

The huge fossilised jaw of a megalodon.

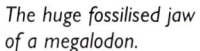

scientists believe it was like a huge, slimmer version of the great white shark.

The megalodon existed at the same time as the helicoprion, which was thought to have had a spiral-toothed mouth. The helicoprion is pictured above.

Blue Shark

The sleek and graceful blue shark is one of the fastest swimmers and one of the greatest travellers. They are found all over the world, from Australia and South Africa to the coasts of North America and the United Kingdom.

Channel Swimmer

The blue sharks of the Atlantic migrate across the oceans each year, following the warm currents of the Gulf Stream up to Europe.

Right: Blue sharks like to eat squid.

Left: The blue shark's long, slim body and snout make it an elegant and powerful swimmer.

Squid Eaters

Their diet consists mostly of squid. Their pointed, serrated teeth are well suited to cope with the slippery, rubbery flesh of their prey.

The streamlined blue shark moves swiftly through the water.

Powerful Swimmer

The blue shark's long, slim body and extra-long caudal fin (the tail) make it a very powerful and elegant swimmer.

A blue shark being tagged by a diver.

FAST FACTS

Location
Worldwide

Habitat
Open water

Size
Up to 3.8 m

Fact
The blue shark is an endangered species due to over-fishing

Hammerhead Shark

The strangely shaped head of the hammerhead makes it the most distinctive of all species of shark. There are nine sub-species of hammerhead and they range in size and colour.

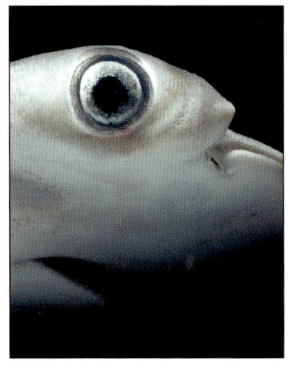

The hammerhead's large eyes provide it with excellent vision.

Great Hammerhead

The largest of all the hammerhead sharks – the great hammerhead – is an extremely menacing predator with a very good sense of smell. It will eat any other fish, squid, octopus and shellfish, but its favourite meal is the stingray. It attacks the ray by holding it down with its hammer and taking bites out of its wings.

Great hammerheads are among the most ferocious of all sharks and attacks on people have been recorded.

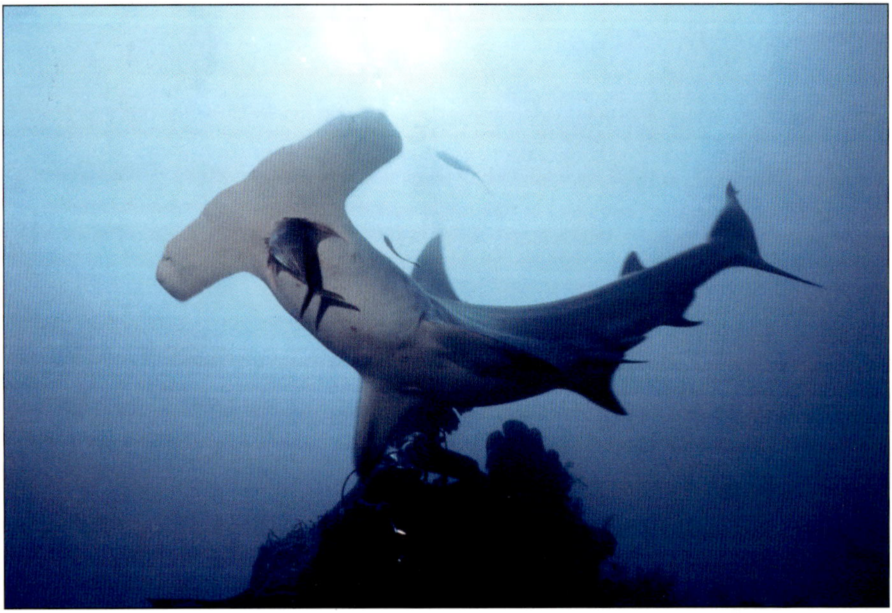

A diver observing a hammerhead shark eating jack fish.

Use Your Head

Experts are yet to discover a reason for such an unusual head. However, with their eyes positioned at either end of the 'hammer', they have good eyesight and can spot their prey very easily. The shape of the head also provides extra 'lift', much like the wings of an aircraft, as it swims through the water.

The hammerhead shark is one of the oddest-looking creatures of the sea.

Sixth Sense

Like all sharks, the hammerhead has the 'sixth sense' that allows it to detect weak electrical signals given out by other sea creatures. The hammerhead has a large number of ampullae of Lorenzini (see page 9) on the sides of its head, which it uses to pick up these signals, and help it to find and catch its prey. Combined with its unusual eyes, the hammerhead is a well-equipped shark.

FAST FACTS

Location
Worldwide, but mostly tropical areas

Habitat
Warm, coastal waters

Size
Up to 6 m

Fact
They eat members of their own species!

Mako sharks are the fastest-swimming sharks and are known to leap clean out of the water.

Fast Swimmers
Scientists have found it difficult to measure the speed of makos, but it is estimated that they can swim at up to 40 km/h. Some have even suggested that they can reach 97 km/h!

Fast Fish
Mako sharks are similar in many ways to another of the world's fastest fish, the tuna. Like tuna, mako sharks make a popular catch for fishermen around the world.

An Even Keel
To reach such speeds, makos have a tail fin that helps them to move through the water. They also have a 'keel' on their underside, to help them change direction.

Gulp!
Its speed allows it to catch other fast fish, such as tuna, mackerel and swordfish.

The streamlined body of the mako shark.

A mako catches up with its prey, bites it hard and swallows it in one gulp. Makos have been known to swallow fish that are about one-sixth of their own body weight.

In Deep Water

Makos prefer deep, cool waters and in the warm Pacific Ocean, they can be found at depths of 200–400 m. On the rare occasions that they come inshore, they can be dangerous to people.

Motoring Along

Mako sharks are so fast, they can easily keep up with a motor boat!

Above: A jaw of a mako shark, with its variety of teeth types.

Left: Its tail fin helps the mako shark to move quickly.

FAST FACTS
Location
Temperate and tropical seas
Habitat
Deep ocean waters
Size
Up to 3.7 m
Fact
Also known as bonito, or blue pointer

Tiger Shark

As its name suggests, the tiger shark is one of the most fearsome sharks in the ocean.

Terrible Teeth
It has razor-sharp, very serrated teeth and can grow to an extremely large size.

Good Sense
Like many killer sharks, tigers have extremely sharp senses. They can detect electric currents in the water, have very good eyesight and a keen sense of smell. A special gill, called a spinacle, behind its eyes helps a tiger shark's

senses. This allows oxygen to flow to the eyes and brain.

Tiger sharks hunt just below the water's surface, and so are often responsible for attacks on people.

Anything Goes

Tiger sharks are well-known for not being fussy eaters. Hunting just beneath the water's surface, they will eat anything, from fish, turtles and other sharks to crabs, shellfish, jellyfish and sea birds. It is not unknown for a tiger shark to eat junk such as tin cans and tyres! Mmmm!

Tiger sharks often hunt for food together (above), and have been known to eat all sorts of rubbish (below).

Stripes and Spots

The tiger shark gets its name from the striped markings

A tiger shark feeding on a marlin carcass.

on its back, rather than from its ferocious reputation. Young tiger sharks have spots, which grow together to form stripes as they get older.

There are three types of thresher sharks – the common thresher, the pelagic thresher and the bigeye thresher.

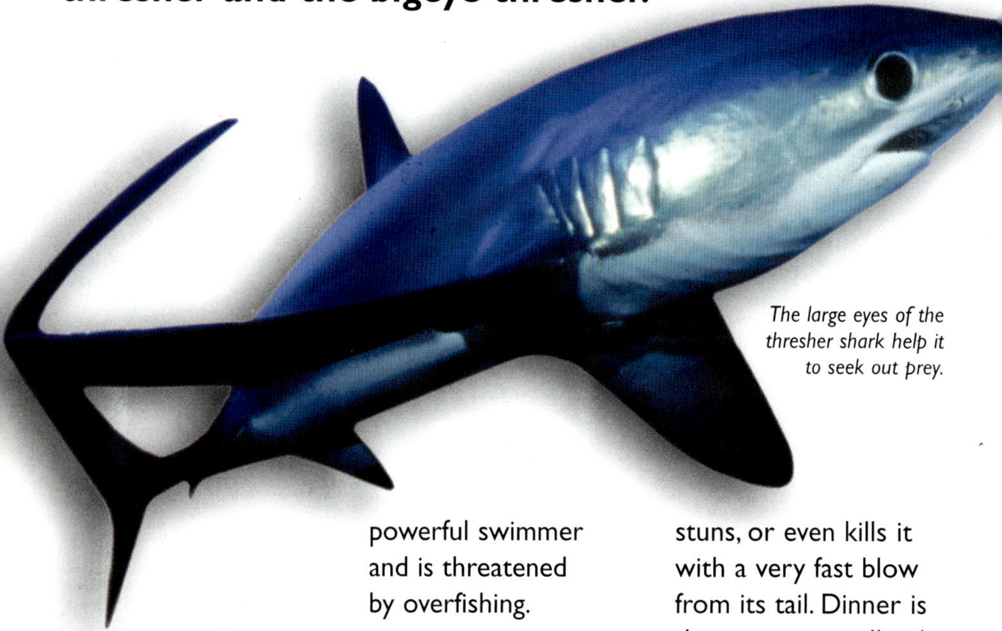

The large eyes of the thresher shark help it to seek out prey.

Long Tail
Their distinctive feature is an extremely long tail fin – the upper part is as long as its body! Like the mako shark (pages 18–19), it is a very powerful swimmer and is threatened by overfishing.

Stunned to Death
The thresher shark gets its name from the way that it uses its tail. To catch and eat its prey, the thresher approaches it and then stuns, or even kills it with a very fast blow from its tail. Dinner is then easy to swallow!

Lunch is Served
Threshers will sometimes hunt in groups, circling large numbers of fish to get an easy meal.

The thresher shark's tail can stun its prey.

Threshers often swim close to the surface, making them a popular catch for sports fishermen.

Killing Power

The killing power of its tail means that it does not need very large teeth and jaws. Of course, being a shark, its teeth are still pretty sharp!

Popular Catch

Thresher sharks are a popular catch for sports fishermen but they are very hard to handle once caught. They have been known to cause serious injuries to fishermen with their tails when pulled on board boats.

Not Aggressive

Threshers are not known to be aggressive towards people, though divers need to be cautious if they get near.

Heavy Babies

The thresher shark gives birth to far fewer pups than other sharks (between only two and six) but the young are much larger. The average length of a thresher shark at birth is 1.5 m.

FAST FACTS

Location
Tropical oceans

Habitat
Coastal, open waters

Size
5 to 6 m

Fact
They are nocturnal

Whale Shark

As its name suggests, the whale shark is very big. In fact, it's the biggest shark (and the biggest fish) in the world!

A whale shark being studied by a diving researcher.

Big Beasts
Adult whale sharks are huge; they're never smaller then 12 m long and can weigh up to 13.2 tonnes.

Gentle Giants
Such a large shark may sound scary, but whale sharks are not at all dangerous – they are true gentle giants. They are quite happy for people to get up close, and divers have even ridden on their backs!

Big Mouth
As you would expect, a really big shark like the whale shark has a very big mouth.

The big and beautiful whale shark has a mouth measuring up to 1.4 m wide.

Measuring up to 1.4 m wide, its mouth is at the very front of its head, rather than underneath, like most other sharks.

Tiny Teeth

Whale sharks have around 3,000 teeth, but they are all very tiny and not used very much. This is because the whale shark is a filter feeder shark. They feed by swimming with their mouths open, taking in huge amounts of seawater and any small creatures in it.

Open Wide... Swallow

The gill slits at the back of its head work like a sieve – letting out water but trapping food in the mouth. When it has a large mouthful of food, it swallows the lot. Whale sharks eat lots of plankton as well as other small fish.

Whale sharks swim with their mouths wide open, sifting the ocean for plankton.

25

Manta Rays

Although they are not strictly sharks, rays are very closely related to them. The largest of all is the manta ray – a scary-looking fish, but in reality, it is one of the gentlest of sea creatures.

The manta ray is a filter feeder, meaning that it waits for food to swim into its jaws.

Devilfish
Fishermen and sailors once thought that the manta ray would swallow boats and people whole. The manta's enormous size and the two 'horns' sticking from the front of its head led to it being called the devilfish, or devil ray.

Toothless
In fact, mantas are harmless filter feeders. They have no teeth and use their 'horns' – types of fins – to funnel plankton into their mouths as they swim along the ocean floor.

The underbelly of the body is mainly white, to hide the manta ray from predators lurking below.

Aquatic Acrobat

To see a manta ray swimming is an incredible sight. They use their 'wings' (types of pectoral fins) to 'fly' through the water. Despite their enormous size, manta rays are quite acrobatic and can sometimes be seen leaping out of the sea. In fact, they have been known to leap 4.5 m out of the water!

Peaceful

Manta rays have few predators. From a young age, they learn to hide themselves by sitting on the sea floor and covering themselves with sand. Even fishermen are not interested in manta rays, so they have a quite a peaceful life!

A manta ray uses its fins to funnel plankton into its mouth.

Manta rays are spectacular to watch.

FAST FACTS

Location
Tropical oceans

Habitat
Coastal, open waters

Size
Up to 9 m

Fact
Also known as the devilfish, or devil ray

The basking shark is the second-largest fish in the world, after the whale shark. Basking sharks get their name because they spend most of their time near the surface, 'basking' in sunshine.

Cruise Control

In fact, it is more likely that basking sharks are at the surface because they are looking for food. Like whale sharks, they are filter feeders — cruising around with their mouths open

Basking sharks love swimming near the surface of the water.

and taking in huge quantities of water and plankton. Basking sharks can process up to 1.5 million litres of water in an hour!

Deep Sleep

They spend the colder parts of the year on the sea floor, though nobody is quite sure why. Some scientists think that they could be in hibernation.

Sea Monsters

Basking sharks often swim together in lines. It is thought that this might have inspired sailors' tales of sea monsters.

The gaping mouth of a basking shark can swallow lots of plankton in one gulp.

The fin of a basking shark, often used in food products.

Basking sharks can reach up to 10 m in length.

Britain and Ireland. Their fins are used to make shark-fin soup and their livers, which can make up a quarter of the shark's weight, are used for oil.

Rough Skin

Basking sharks spend a lot of time close to the shore, either alone or in large groups. They are often seen by people and are not at all dangerous. Their skin however, is very rough and can injure swimmers.

Shark-fin Soup

Basking sharks are fished wherever they are found, including around the coasts of

FAST FACTS
Location
Temperate waters
Habitat
Coastal areas, near the water's surface
Size
Up to 10 m
Fact
Also known as the sunfish

White Tip Reef Shark

You are most likely to find the white tip reef shark around Pacific Ocean coral reefs, such as those off the coast of Australia.

White Tips

White tips are quite small, slender and dark grey in colour. The dorsal fin – on its back – and the caudal fins – its tail fin – have white tips. That is where their name comes from.

White tips hiding under a rock.

Standing Still

During the day, white tips spend their time in sea caves or similar places in a coral reef. In a large cave,

White tips swim around the sea floor at night looking for food.

White tips spend a lot of time in caves, looking for food.

many white tips will gather together, 'stacked' on top of one another like logs! They may also remain perfectly still on the sea bottom for long periods of time.

Night Lovers

White tips are most active at night, when they swim around the reefs or sea floor searching for food.

They are excellent at finding food in holes, under ledges and other hideaways.

Rarely Aggressive

They are not great travelers, and will stay in the same area for months or years. Despite this, they do not guard their territory and are very rarely aggressive. They will often take food offered to them by divers.

FAST FACTS

Location
Tropical waters

Habitat
Sea bottom in coastal areas, near coral reefs

Size
Up to 2.1 m

Fact
Often on the sea bed searching for food

31

Probably the most famous and feared of all sharks, the great white is the ocean's most ferocious predator.

Feared and Ferocious

Despite being so well known, great whites are rarely seen and they are not yet fully understood.

Big Appetite

Great whites will eat pretty much anything they can get their jaws on. Their preferred meals are large fish, other sharks, sea birds, seals and sea lions – anything that's big enough to satisfy their appetite.

Man-eater

They have been known to eat people, but thankfully, this is quite rare. It is thought that a great white can go without food for up to two months after a big meal.

Terrible Teeth

This fearsome fish is well-equipped for hunting. The great white has around 3,000 teeth at any one time. They are triangular, serrated, razor-sharp and up to 7.5 cm long.

The nose is made of cartilage, which is less fragile than bone and can withstand much damage.

The white belly of the great white helps it blend in with the sky above.

Fast Swimmer

The great white's streamlined shape and pointed snout make a fast swimmer for a shark of its size. They can swim at up to 24 km/h.

A great white shark attacks a Cape fur seal, by butting it from underneath.

Camouflaged

Only the great white's underbelly is white – it's grey on top. This makes it very hard to spot them from below and makes it easier for them to sneak up and catch their prey.

Hunting Prey

Great whites have very sensitive ampullae of Lorenzini to detect electrical currents in the water. They also have a great sense of smell – they can detect one drop of blood in 4,600,000 litres of water.

Great whites often attack the protective cages of diving researchers.

FAST FACTS

Location
Temperate waters

Habitat
Coastal areas

Size
Up to 7 m

Fact
It was made famous by the film *Jaws*

Dogfish

There are several types of dogfish sharks. Relatively small, dogfish are the most common shark in the world. They are often caught and used by people for food and oil.

The skin of a dogfish is rough and spiny.

Poisonous Spines

The spiny dogfish is the most common of all. It is grey with white spots and is known for the sharp spines on its back. These are used to protect it from predators as it spends its time searching for food on the sea bottom. The spines contain a mild poison, which can cause a nasty wound if handled.

Travelling Band

They are called dogfish because they travel and hunt in large schools. These groups are often made up of dogfish of the same age or sex, and can

Dogfish are well camouflaged. Their colours hide them amongst the plants and rocks of the ocean.

sometimes contain thousands of individuals.

if you have ever eaten fish and chips, it's quite likely that you have eaten dogfish and chips!

A greater spotted dogfish looking for food.

FAST FACTS

Location
Temperate waters

Habitat
Coastal areas

Size
Up to 1.2 m

Fact
The most common type of shark

Shark Sandwich

As the most common type of shark, it is also the one that is most eaten by people. In Britain, it is often sold as 'rock salmon' so

Tiny Baby

Baby dogfish are tiny, rarely reaching more than 10 cm in length.

Look out for those poisonous spines!

No one is sure how nurse sharks came by their name, but they do make a sucking sound a bit like a baby!

The nurse shark has barbels to help it locate potential prey.

are shaped a bit like a fan and are designed to be able to crush the hard shells of the prey that it eats.

Smooth Skin

Nurse sharks are a dark grey-brown colour and sometimes have spots. Unlike many sharks, a nurse shark's skin is smooth to touch. They have a wide head and very strong jaws.

Social Sharks

Nurse sharks are large, slow-moving and known as one of the most social of all sharks because they are always in groups.

Fan Teeth

They live mainly on the sea bottom, where they feed on shrimp, lobster, crabs and any other shellfish. The nurse shark's teeth

Whiskers

The most distinctive thing about a nurse shark's appearance is

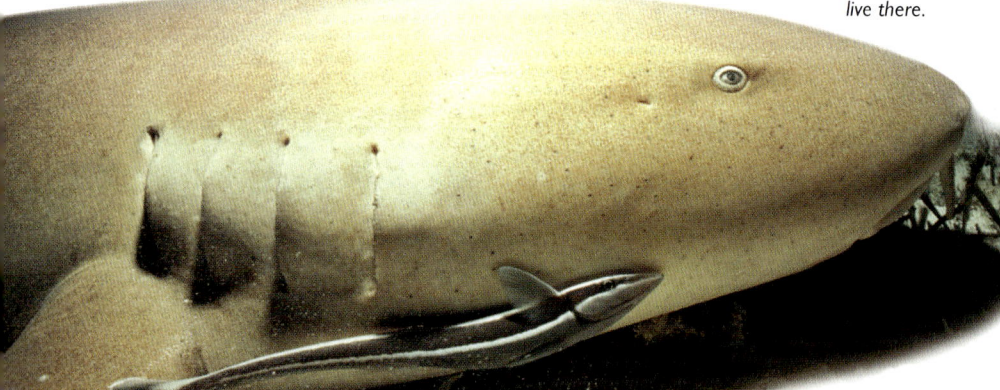

Nurse sharks usually live on the sea bottom, feeding on the creatures which live there.

It's possible for divers to get very close to nurse sharks.

the two whisker-like barbels on its upper jaw. These thin, fleshy organs help them to touch and taste when they are feeding.

Nursing School

As well as living together in large schools nurse sharks generally stay in the same place. During the day they will stay together on the sea bottom, piled up on top of one another.

Captive

Nurse sharks do well when kept in captivity, so you may see one up close if you visit an aquarium or sea life centre.

Nurse sharks are slow-moving and graceful.

The leopard shark is so named because of its markings of dark brown spots on a silver background.

A leopard shark blends in well with the rocky sea bed.

Camouflage

The leopard shark changes its skin colour to adapt to its environment. This helps it to hide in areas of coral – a good source of food – and rock. When a shark dies, its body decomposes to form coral for the next generations.

Diet

The leopard shark lives on a diet of worms, clams, crabs, shrimps, octopuses and other small fish found at the bottom of the sea. It uses its sharp teeth to capture these animals.

The leopard shark lies in wait for prey by resting on the bottom of the ocean.

The skin of a leopard shark looks scaly, very much like that of a fish.

Babies

The female leopard shark produces an egg which is kept inside the body. When the egg hatches, the shark then gives birth. She can give birth to as many as 30 pups in one litter. An animal that reproduces in this way is called ovoviviparous.

Age

The leopard shark lives to be about 30 years old. Males reach adulthood between the ages of seven and thirteen, and females between ten and fifteen.

A distinctively marked leopard shark.

FAST FACTS

Location
Pacific coast of North America

Habitat
Bays, near the shore

Size
Up to 2 m

Fact
Very shy and not considered a threat to humans

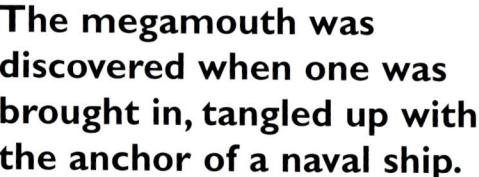

Megamouth

The megamouth was discovered when one was brought in, tangled up with the anchor of a naval ship.

Discovery
The first megamouth was discovered in 1976 off the coast of Hawaii. Since the discovery, scientists have struggled to find out more about these fascinating creatures.

The megamouth can grow to 5 m long.

Slow Movers
The big megamouth is slow-moving and it is thought that they do not travel great distances.

Rubber Lips
The megamouth's body is rounded. With thick, rubbery lips and widely-spaced eyes on a very large head (almost as long as the main part of its body), it is certainly an unusual-looking creature.

The huge mouth of the megamouth shark is rarely photographed.

Big Mouth

The most distinctive feature of the megamouth shark is its mouth, which is …well, mega-big! At up to 1 m across, it uses this huge mouth to scoop up large amounts of plankton and other small creatures near the surface at night.

Glowing Lips

Only a few megamouths have been found and very little is known about them. Scientists

The megamouth's 'glowing' lips.

cannot agree about its 'glowing lips'. Some say that the megamouth uses them to attract larger prey close to its mouth, while others think that its mouth reflects light from the luminous things it eats.

More Mystery

There may be other mysterious creatures lurking in the oceans.

FAST FACTS

Location
Warm oceans

Habitat
Deep sea areas

Size
Up to 5 m

Fact
First discovered off the coast of Hawaii in 1976

Lemon Shark

The deep yellow colour along the back of the lemon shark helps to explain its name. It is one of the most studied sharks in the world.

Attracted to Colour

Lemon sharks are commonly found near the water surface in bays, docks and river mouths. They have been known to attack people if disturbed or provoked and it is thought that they

A lemon shark being studied.

could be attracted to the bright colours of swimming costumes and safety equipment.

Easy to Study

Despite this, many have been brought into captivity and studied by scientists. Unlike many species of shark, lemon sharks do not need to keep swimming in order to breathe, which makes them fairly easy to study.

Shake

Whilst all sharks shed their teeth and grow new ones, lemon sharks do it more

A diver takes a close look at a lemon shark.

A young lemon shark out on the prowl.

The lemon shark has a very streamlined shape.

close to the area in which they were born, hiding from predators and feeding on fish. With age, they move further offshore.

often than any other, gaining a new set every 7–8 days! Its teeth are long, thin and very sharp. When it catches prey, it shakes its head very quickly to break it up.

Hideaway

When lemon sharks are young, they stay

FAST FACTS

Location
Warm oceans

Habitat
Coastal areas

Size
Up to 3.1 m

Fact
Most common off the coast of Florida, USA

Bull Shark

As their name suggests, bull sharks are large, aggressive and are thought to attack people quite often. However, they do not have horns!

Fresh Water

Bull sharks are very common in the world's warm and tropical oceans and spend a lot of time close to the shore. They are also able to survive for

Bull sharks may be sensitive to low-frequency sounds created by movement.

long periods of time in fresh water. Because of this they are common visitors to estuaries, rivers and lakes.

FAST FACTS

Location
Warm oceans

Habitat
Coastal areas

Size
Up to 3.5 m

Fact
One of the most dangerous sharks in the world

Travelling Far

Bull sharks have been found as far as 2,800 km up the Mississippi River in the USA and 4,000 km up the Amazon River in Peru. They have also been seen in inland lakes in Africa and South America.

Bull sharks have been sighted in the freshwater of the Mississippi and Amazon rivers.

Shark Attack

Bull sharks will attack and eat almost anything, including people. The large numbers of bull sharks and the fact that they live near coasts helps to explain why they are responsible for so many shark attacks.

Some experts believe that bull sharks are sensitive to low-frequency sounds in the water, created by movement. Try to keep still if you see one!

Bull sharks often travel in shallow water close to the shore (above), and look very fearsome (below).

Shark Attacks

Shark attacks on people are actually very rare – only about 100 attacks are reported around the world each year and very few of these end in the victim being killed.

Surfers

Sharks will attack people if they feel threatened or if they mistake someone in the water for their usual prey. Surfers off the coasts of Australia and California are particularly at risk from shark attacks. To a shark, a surfer paddling on a surfboard, with their arms and legs in the water, may look very much like a seal.

A diver wearing chain mail to protect against shark bites.

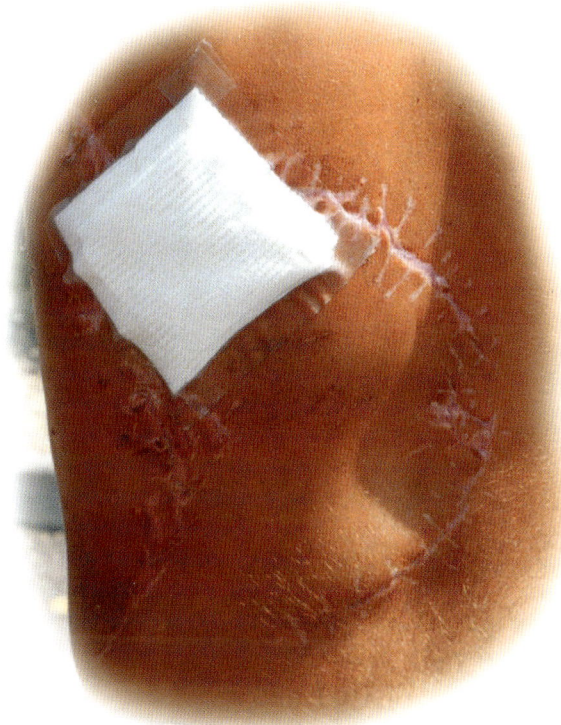

The shape of a shark's jaw is clearly visible on this man's back.

Eaten

One famous shark attack occurred during the Second World War. The *USS Indianapolis* was sunk, leaving over 1,000 men in the water. Rescuers arrived to find only 117 survivors who reported that their crewmates had all been eaten by sharks!

Electric Fence

In places where sharks are common and people spend time in the water, safe areas are enclosed by nets. Experiments have been carried out with a type of 'electric fence' to keep the sharks away from the people.

Keep Still

Lifeguards on the beach keep an eye out and advice is given about what to do should you find yourself face to snout with a shark. This includes remaining as still as possible and punching the shark on the snout to put it off biting you!

Killer Species

Of the 350 shark species, only 32 are known to have attacked human beings.

Both the board and the surfer came off badly here.

Glossary

Ampullae of Lorenzini Pores on the side of sharks' heads to pick up electrical signals.

Basking Lying in the sun.

Chainmail Flexible armour made of metal rings or links.

Elasmobranch Family to which sharks, manta rays, skates, guitarfish and sawfish belong.

Endangered In danger of extinction.

Filter feeders Sea creatures that feed by filtering plankton from the water.

Fossilised Preserved in rock or shell.

Hibernation A long sleep, generally lasting the whole winter.

Luminous Glowing, reflecting or radiating light.

Migrate Journey to a warmer climate for the winter.

Oviparous Sharks that produce eggs that hatch outside the body.

Ovoviviparous Sharks that grow inside an egg inside the female shark's body.

Nocturnal Most active at night.

Plankton Tiny sea creatures and plant material.

Predator A creature that hunts others on which to feed.

School A large group of sharks.

Serrated Saw-like, as in a shark's teeth.

Species A group of creatures sharing common features.

Spiracle A gill slit.

Streamlined Shaped to move easily through the water.

Temperate A climate that is neither too hot nor too cold.

Viviparous Sharks that give birth to live young, called pups.

Acknowledgements

Key: Top - t; middle - m; bottom - b; left - l; right - r; NPL - Naturepl.com; NSP - Natural Science Photos.

Cover: Digital Stock. **1:** Jeff Rotman/npl. **2:** (t) Jeff Rotman/npl; (m) TTAT; (b) Jeff Rotman/NPL. **3:** (t,b) Digital Stock. **4:** (t) Jeff Rotman/NPL; (b) Corel. **5:** (t) Paul Kay/NSP. **6:** Mike Atkinson. **7:** (t) Corel. **8:** (t) Digital Stock; (b) Corel. **9:** Digital Stock. **10:** Brandon Cole/NPL. **11:** (tl) James D. Watt/Seapics.com; (tr) Jeff Rotman/NPL; (bottom: tl,tr,br) Georgette Douwma/Science Photo Library; (bl) Top That!. **12:** (l) Top That!; (r) Steve White. **13:** (tr) Jeff Rotman/NPL; (m,b) Steve White. **14:** (t) Corel; (b) Bob Cranston/NSP. **15:** Digital Stock. **16:** (t) Jeff Rotman NPL; (b) Gary J. Adkison/Seapics.com. **17:** Jeff Rotman/NPL. **18:** Digital Stock. **19:** (t,b) Bob Cranston/NSP; (m) Ken Hoppen/NSP. **20:** Jeff Rotman/NPL. **21:** (t) Bob Cranston/NSP; (m) Top That!; (b) Ben Cropp Productions / Seapics.com. **22:** Jason Isley/Scubazoo.com. **23:** Scott Tuason/imagequest3d.com. **24:** Digital Stock; **25:** (t) James D.Watt/Seapics.com; (b) Bob Cranston/NSP. **26:** (t) Digital Stock; (b) Corel. **27:** (t) Masa Ushioda/Seapics.com; (b) Corel. **28:** (t) Dan Burton/NPL; (b) Jeff Rotman/NPL. **29:** Dan Burton/NPL. **30:** Digital Stock. **31:** Corel. **32:** James D.Watt/Seapics.com. **33:** (t,m) Digital Stock; (b) C&M Fallows/seapics.com. **34:** (t) Alan James/NPL; (b) Paul Kay/NSP. **35:** (t) D P Wilson/FLPA; (b) Paul Kay/NSP **36:** (t) Bob Cranston/NSP; (b)Jeff Rotman/NPL. **37:** (t) Corel; (b) Francis Abbott/NPL. **38:** (t) Hal Beral/NSP; (b) Hemera. **39:** (t) Hal Beral/NSP; (b) R. Austin/FLPA. **40:** John Butler. **41:** Bruce Rasner/ Rotman/NPL. **42:** (t) Bob Shanley/Rex Features; (b) Digital Stock. **43:** (t) Masa Ushioda/Imagequest3d.com; (b) Jeff Rotman/NPL. **44:** Brandon Cole/NPL. **45:** (t,b) Jeff Rotman/NPL; (m) Brandon Cole/NPL. **46:** (t) Digital Vision; (b) Corel. **47:** (t) Rex Features; (b) South West News Service/Rex features.